Warsaw. The sleepi~~~~
awakening. After suffering the v~~~~
century, from absolute destructio~~~~
of repression, the rebuilt patchw~~~~
with energy.

Its beauty might be unconventional, but Warsaw's riches lie elsewhere. Interactive museums and fresh art tackle the past with sensitivity. Chefs reinterpret traditional cuisine; sweeping parks are alive with art and music. Even the Palace of Science and Culture —Stalin's "gift" to the Polish people—has been reclaimed with cinemas, theatres, libraries and clubs.

Sharing their side to Warsaw are a few local legends: the godfather of Polish techno, a leading fashion designer, an architect and dramatist couple and a photographer who's found success abroad but still prefers home. A feature pits commercialism against culture, a short story portrays a nocturnal scene, and a photo showcase treads the boundaries of society. It's all about original minds and the creative vibe. Get lost in the sights, flavours and sounds of the city. Get lost in Warsaw.

Photo: A. Savin

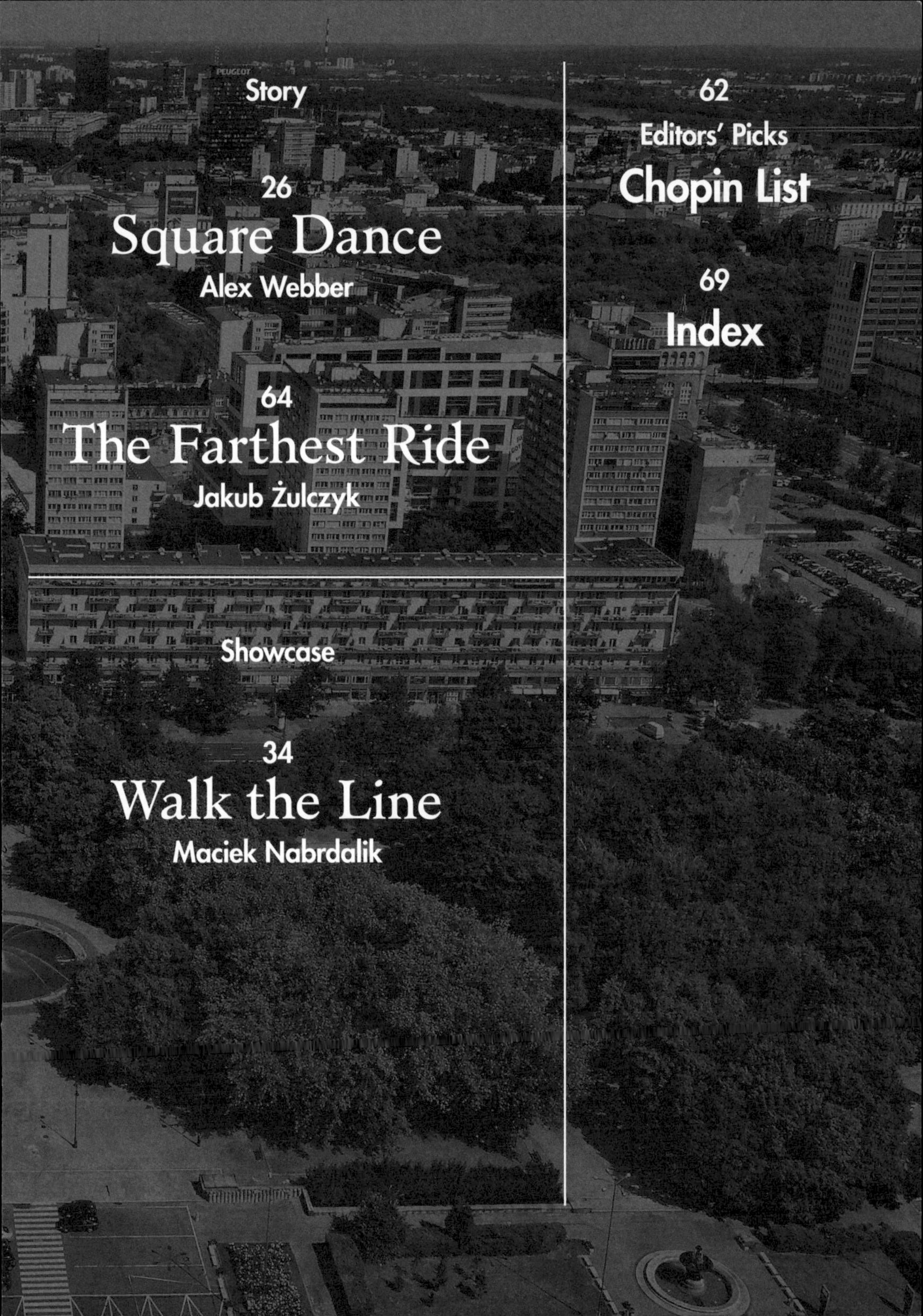

Warsaw's Vistula River has traditionally marked the boundary between two distinct cities, each with their own identity: while the left bank was turned into rubble by the Second World War, the right bank, Praga, emerged relatively unscathed. Ponder the reconstructed Old Town in front and the other facets of the surrounding patchwork in the honey of a summer sunset.
• Vistula River Beach, Praga

Warsaw clubbers fall into two groups: those who adore *Nowa Jerozolima*—and those too creeped out to enter the former children's hospital. Yet despite its murky origins, the atmosphere is electrifying. Poles are some of the loveliest revellers around, and you're bound to share vodkas with new friends before dancing all night under the coloured-lit windows of this remarkable space. If your body and soul craves further dancing, notorious after-party *Luzztro* can serve you up a more intensive course of treatment.
• Nowa Jerozolima, Aleje Jerozolimskie 57; Luzztro, Aleje Jerozolimskie 6, Centre

From Communist Diners to a Revolutionary Design House

Back to Life

Few places in Europe offer two wholesome courses for under a fiver. That makes Warsaw's "milk bars" worth a visit—along with the spectacle of yuppies eating beside the jobless and elderly. Gentrification closed many "bar mleczny", and *Prasowy* (pictured) was only saved after an uproar. These institutions—try *Bambino* too—are no longer state-run, but the canteen vibe persists. Queues allow time to interpret the menu. And the pierogi, chicken soup and "gołąbki" rolls will make you think you've acquired a new Polish mother.
• Centre, various locations,
see Index p. 64

Outdoors · Culture   Green Gallery

Warsaw's Museum of Modern Art might not yet have a permanent home, but it's still highly active from a space at Pańska 3, another soon to be opened in Powiśle, and other offshoots spreading life around the city. *Bródno Sculpture Park* has revitalised the residential district of Targówek, thanks in part to Polish creator Paweł Althamer. He enlisted local children to help plant a small botanical garden there. With a multiple-sclerosis sculpture group, he also produced a fountain shaped like a woman whose breasts gush water.

Pictured is Monika Sosnowska's "Lattice"—inspired by bars and rails observed in the neighbourhood. Look out for Olafur Eliasson's skilfully concealed "Reverse Ice Kaleidoscope". And don't try to locate Ai Weiwei's "To Be Found": fragments of replicas of an ancient Chinese vase buried in the park. Invisible and untouchable, it speaks of history and identity; the fragments a powerful reminder of Warsaw's destruction and reconstruction.
• Bródno Sculpture Park, Bródno, artmuseum.pl

Standing at the crossroads between propaganda, marketing and street art is the poster. And the humble, democratic medium goes way back in Poland, where a famous wave of artists forever changed the face of graphic design. It's understandable, then, that Warsaw has its own *Poster Museum* (Muzeum Plakatu). Design fans should think nothing of the trip south, to the end of many a bus line. It's worth it to explore the small exhibition space, displaying some of the most iconic creations from the last decades, as well as a review of more modern takes. Grab takeaway graphics at the gift shop before moving on to the adjacent Wilanów Palace. Set among gorgeous grounds, it also contains a restaurant famous for reprising long-forgotten Polish recipes.

• Poster Museum, Stanisława Kostki Potockiego 10/16, postermuseum.pl

As far as Slavic gods go, Weles is pretty busy, with the earth, fertility, medicine and magic on his list. No wonder he needs a stylish cocktail bar to relax in. And what a beauty he had built for him. With imported zinc ceilings and a bar made of an old carousel, *Weles* looks like it's fallen out of time—unlike the innovative cocktails and friendly staff. Try the Pornstar Martini, coming with a champagne shot. You deserve it for finding this divine wonder, hidden in a courtyard behind an inconspicuous black door.

• Weles Bar, Nowogrodzka 11, welesbar.pl

Culture **Space to Think**

Active in the Polish underground during the war, friend to Le Corbusier, Picasso and Henry Moore... Finnish-born Oskar Hansen, who became a Polish citizen in the 1920s, was a giant in sculpture, design and architecture. His principal concept was "Open Form"—the idea of "shaping the cognitive space" and integrating humans with their environment. But under a repressive government many of his ideas were not realised, and he was even put on trial for his design of a city hall for Warsaw. His purest creation is perhaps the *Oskar Hansen House* just outside the capital in Szumin, built with his wife Zofia. Visits organised by the Museum of Modern Art display his concepts in action, with an innovative blending of interior and exterior spaces.
• Oskar Hansen House, Mlekicie 4, Szumin, artmuseum.pl

Food **Fine Line**

Nolita is all about balance. The intimate interior manages to strike the sweet spot between formal and casual. And in the same way, the exceptional cuisine touches fine dining while satisfying the base urge to be truly well fed. Chef Jacek Grochowina shows enough to interest the folks at Michelin—one possible dish might be an assiette of tomatoes, presenting the complex fruit in a bewildering variety of forms. But he also sends you home with every sense sated: flair and originality in the main courses never come at the expense of a large morsel to sink your teeth into. A five-course tasting menu is available with optional paired wines.
• Nolita, Wilcza 46, Centre, nolita.pl

Ania Kuczyńska
She studied haute couture in
Italy and Paris before returning
to her hometown to launch
her eponymous clothing line.
Since her first show in
an underground car park,
her designs have become
ubiquitous among Warsaw's
most fashionable denizens

Ania Kuczyńska, Fashion Designer

Black and White

Ania Kuczyńska is a self-professed Warsaw girl, born and raised.
Here, the monochrome maven explains what the city's about and
points us to good art and heavy techno

Your clothing is described as Warsaw in textile form. Is that on purpose?

I've always been a Warsaw girl and it's what comes naturally. The palette of colours is very appropriate for the city. I'd describe myself as an Eastern designer, in a good sense—I'm very influenced by and inspired by colours and surroundings. My childhood was pretty grey, the weather here is grey, the sky is grey and the buildings were grey. So there's lots of grey and black and that comes out in my projects and collections. My next collection is called East because of inspiration from here, Asia and traditional Polish culture. Doing collections and drawing projects is a mix of many experiences. What's important for me is that it is authentic—that my emotions come out through what I am doing.

How would you describe Warsaw?

Warsaw is a very strange city. It's not like falling in love at first sight. It's not beautiful, it's not in the heart of Europe. What I like is that we have such a rich history —from wars to Communism— and Warsaw is a mix of it. The architecture is not obvious; it's a fascinating mix of a lot of styles and influences. Warsaw is also a very energetic city, even though it's hectic. It's energetic in a good way—very inspiring. If you want to really get into the vibe of Warsaw you have to experience very different things. There's alternative scenes, glamorous ones, all types of people. For me it's always been super cool that you never know where you're going to find what you like. People here are still hungry, still discovering—they still want to build things. That's what I like about my city.

We're meeting in Mokotów: is this where you live?

This is my hood, but I grew up in Śródmieście which is the centre. For me it was really interesting because I lived in an old prewar building, a beautiful apartment with ornate old heaters that were a different colour in every room. The building still had holes from the Second World War. That's what Warsaw is like—it's full of these moments that influence you.

And how is Mokotów different?

Mokotów is very residential, it's easygoing, and it's large. Warsaw is not a place where you have a clear definition of what the centre is—the city is actually very big, and there are areas I've never been to. Everyone creates their own little centre of life and their own map.

And what's on your Mokotów map?

I like to go for coffee at *Kawiarnia Relaks* and nearby there's a great Mexican place called *Gringo Bar*. The falafel place *Mezze* also has very fresh and tasty food.

Where do you go when you need to take your mind off work?

I like museums. *The National Museum* is in a very interesting building; the architecture is monumental and the collection is great. I also like *Skaryszewski Park* on the other side of the river. It's very beautiful and you can really get lost in there. *Zachęta* is also one of my favourite museums, the building itself is beautiful and they show very good contemporary art.

Speaking of lost, what's the best way to get lost in Warsaw?

I like parties—I love "Brutaż", which is a super cool techno party that's always thrown in different places, the music there is usually good. Artur8 always throws great

One young, fresh gallery on the Warsaw scene is Pola Magnetyczne, attractive for more than just its name

Luzztro
Centre

Mysia-3
Centre

Red Onion
Muranów

MOKO61
Centre

Zoo Market
Praga

Super Salon
Centre

parties as well with "King of Kong". Check them out on Facebook. I like to get lost that way, by dancing. I'm more of a techno girl. There is also a super cool hardcore club called *Luzztro*. You can party all night and then in the morning cross the street to the National Museum! The scene is getting better and better; there are lots of places where people are coming to play.

You've clearly got an eye for good design and quality—where do you go for some retail therapy?

I like Nap and She/s A Riot in the concept department store *Mysia-3*, both those stores are nice. I also like *Red Onion*, as well as *MOKO61* for sunglasses, *Zoo Market* for vintage shopping and *Super Salon* for magazines.

Are there any local designers you're excited about?

I really love the brand UEG. I was a co-founder and in the beginning it was mostly clothes made of Tyvek. It's an outstanding brand in that it's very characteristic. The clothing is all black and white, very curated and minimalistic. There's lots of zip-ups and hoodies and it's very popular with rappers right now. It's cool because it has a message. I like the jewellery brand Pak; they're doing very beautiful rings and bracelets. There's also a girl who makes headbands I really love, Cosima Burowska. She comes from an aristocratic family from Florence and moved here in the 1980s. She studied embroidery in Italy and now makes really charismatic and interesting headbands.

From your shows to the collaboration with legendary designer Karol Śliwka, your brand has always had a special relationship with art—where can we find interesting art in the city?

I think *Galeria Raster* is doing really interesting things. I also like *Piktogram* in Praga, run by Michał Wolinski. He's a really interesting person and they're doing great things. There's also the *Kasia Michalski* gallery, she just had a show of Agnieszka Brzeżańska photos and paintings which was beautiful. There's also this cool couple—he's French and she's Polish—and they run a fantastic gallery called *Pola Magnetyczne*. And *Fundacja Arton* showcases mostly conceptual art by forgotten or unknown creators, with a big focus on female artists. Now they're doing an exhibition in an old printing factory in Warsaw, a very interesting space that's totally abandoned.

Are there any bars you like to go to?

Weles is a very beautiful bar. You go down these dark stairs and there's a chandelier and it's all perfect. They make absolutely amazing drinks.

Where do you nip out for lunch during work sessions downtown?

For coffee or a quick something *Zorza* is great, plus *Przegryź* across the street from my shop. Lots of people love that place, it's very popular and a nice local spot. I love the food there—it's mostly Polish cuisine. There's also a super cool vegan sushi place called *Youmiko*.

Where do you eat when you have something to celebrate?

There's one place called *Nolita*. It's very special, but not even that expensive because you can have a five-course menu for about 50 euros per person. It's a fantastic and deep culinary experience. The place is quite intimate and I like that it's discreet. I like places that aren't pretentious. There's another place in a courtyard off Mokotowska called *Alewino*, where you can have a wonderful meal with very good wine. There's two waiters—the younger guy with dark hair and one with glasses. It's good to grab them, they know their wines and will recommend something great.

Where do you take friends when they come to visit?

There's a wonderful restaurant called *U Kucharzy*—it used to be in a much better location but it's still quite good. I would suggest anyone coming to town to try different things—there's the old *Hala Mirowska* market, the new Zoo Market and *Olympia*. There's also the *Nocny Market* ("Night Market"), which has loads of food stalls. Things are moving and changing all the time here. You also should not miss the chain *Lukullus* —they make their own pastries from old recipes and use real butter for everything.

The city is changing rapidly— what changes would you like to see in Warsaw?

Politics. Unfortunately the bad wind has come and there's something wrong happening in Poland.

The environment might be neo-classical, but the exhibits are cutting-edge at Zachęta National Gallery of Art

Urban Mosaic

Mokotów is the epitome of Warsaw's rapid change: the leafy zone studded with socialist architecture has flowered with atmospheric cafés, fine dining spots and boutiques alongside vintage stores

| Outdoors · Culture | **Royal Treatment**

The easiest way to get lost in Warsaw might be to enter one of numerous gates into its largest park, *Łazienki*. Mokotów's 76-hectare green lung was 18th-century king Stanisław August's summer residence. And among the grounds you'll soon stumble upon attractions that reflect the king's passions of philosophy and art—five different gardens, historical buildings now serving as museums, an amphitheatre circled by 16 carved poets and playwrights, and the Palace on the Isle (pictured) still containing its original baroque baths ("łazienki"). A massive monument to Fredrik Chopin is a replica of its original, destroyed by the Nazis during World War II. A year after it was replaced, a summer tradition of weekly piano recitals began there—still to this day enjoyed by locals, visitors, and even the resident peacocks.

• Łazienki Park, Aleje Ujazdowskie, Ujazdów

Odd Couple

It might seem strange to specialise in two such contrasting foods as ramen and donuts. But your doubts will be dispelled by a simple taste of either. The reason is plain and simple—these are just two things the folk at *Mod* are really, really good at. The ramen are delicious homemade noodles cooked sous vide—and this difficult system reaps big rewards, especially in their super spicy tantanmen. Meanwhile the homemade donuts, in flavours like hibiscus and matcha, are phenomenal: especially when it comes to the wonder of the donut ice cream sandwich. If choosing is tricky—just have it all.
• Mod, Oleandrów 8, Mokotów

Hearty Mouthful

The flip side of the milk bar—where you can have a Christmas feast for loose change—is the new phase of Varsovian chefs touting themselves to Michelin by moleculising ingredients and presenting dishes that resemble a 3D Kandinsky painting. *Papu*, however, offers a heartier take on the upgrading of true-blue Polish cuisine. Here, the cabbage rolls are stuffed with locally sourced lamb, the pierogi are plumped up with pheasant and the bottle-lined walls present a cultured mouthful of a different variety.
• Papu, Aleja Niepodległości 132/136, Mokotów, restauracjapapu.pl

Rebooted Design

Standing between Mokotów's thrift shops and its sleek concept stores is *Reset*. The selection runs through quirk, kitsch, retro and modern—with all products made by local hands. Browse the immaculate vignettes for hand-printed notebooks, colourful furniture and inventive takes on homeware like step ladders and stools. Large-scale maps of Warsaw make a better souvenir than a lousy t-shirt—though they might be trumped by a giant pierogi-shaped cushion. And when you've dropped enough zlotys, pop next door for a poster exhibition and a good cup of coffee.
• Reset Art&Design Point, Puławska 48, Mokotów, resetpoint.pl

Culture — Staging the New

Poland has a grand theatrical and cinematic tradition, and the edgiest modern incarnation might just be found at *Nowy Teatr*. The driving force is director Krzysztof Warlikowski, whose productions have garnered praise on an international level. On home turf, his concept has generally been breaking down the fourth wall and inviting audience members to contribute— and join a living, breathing discussion to effect social change. Look out for visits from international theatre companies—and even the occasional opera. Performances are offered in English.

• Nowy Teatr, Madalińskiego 10/16, Mokotów, nowyteatr.org/en

Culture · Food — Labyrinth of Wonder

Unpretentious is the best way to describe this joint. Amble through the front garden and work your way through each room of a former military office—still with its pre-war wood-panelled staircase and carved balustrades—until you find what you're looking for. On some nights, a room hosting an indie gig—on others, a balcony full of swing dancers. The back garden lends itself to daytime picnics and grills, and nighttime soul explosions. With its easygoing vibe, decent drinks list and menu with plenty for veggies—*Dzik* is an institution for the people.

• Dzik, Belwederska 44a, Ujazdów

Shop — Japandinavia

The passion of Zuzanna and Alexander has given way to a crisp oasis of creativity on a calm side street. *Thisispaper* sells original backpacks hand-crafted in the studio on-site, and exhibited gallery-style in a space peppered with cactuses, art books and exquisite magazines—including the in-house publication. They also bottle their own home-brewed varieties of green tea, to warm you against the Polish winter or refresh you from the punishing summer. Sip and chat to the friendly staff on their artistic perspective on the city.

• Thisispaper, Odolańska 6/8, Mokotów, thisispapershop.com

| Night | Potato Head |

Poland is historically a nation of vodka drinkers, and a short time in Warsaw will see you quaff more than you have since before you knew better. But beyond the famous bison grass Żubrówka, there's plenty to discover in a rapidly developing market. A good starting point for your spiritual journey is among the quiet residential streets of Mokotów. *Bar Wieczorny* is manned by a couple of mixologists as wise as they are pleasant— definitely a recurring theme in Warsaw. Among the varieties of potato elixir is a particular one of interest—Młody Ziemniak. Only distilled once, it cannot legally be classified as vodka in the EU. And the flavour is a revelation: you can actually taste the young potatoes from which it is made. What's more, each year has its own distinct profile thanks to varying weather conditions, noted scrupulously on the bottle. And the bartenders at Wieczorny even picked some of the spuds with their own hands. Non-purists can also enjoy a variety of sours and an assortment of creative cocktails. Enjoy your drinks and nibbles under the fairy lights and fruit trees in the building's court- yard—with the Communist architecture looming overhead. And when you manage to rouse yourself, the staff will even suggest where you should go next.

• Bar Wieczorny, Wiśniowa 46, Mokotów

Line In

Jacek Sienkiewicz
He started DJing in the early 1990s and became a trail-blazer for the Polish electronic music scene since. He runs the label Recognition Records and has just released his new album "Hideland". It might be his last full-on techno album, as he dabbles his feet in different melodic waters

Warsaw and its club scene have been undergoing a constant make-over during the past twenty years. Part of it from day one, Jacek has a good vantage point on the what and what nots of the city's nightlife. He takes us on a tour through wide green spaces and ponders the flawed beauty of his hometown

You travel a lot as a DJ, so what makes Warsaw special to you?

Well, my relationship with Warsaw is a bit shaky. I tried a couple of times to move away for good. There were times when I said to myself, I don't know why I'm still here. I moved to Berlin twice and once to Kraków but I always end up back here. The jokey answer would be, it's because we have beautiful girls and good cheap food. But obviously Warsaw is more than that. It's not a city you fall in love with at first sight. If you're here for only 24 hours it could be a boring, or even disgusting experience, because it's basically many cities attached to each other and it's hard to figure out where to go and where not. Take the area around the Palace of Culture, directly in the so called "Centre". Of course the palace is amazing and interesting, but everything around it is just bleak— empty and boring. But once you break through that surface, you'll find out how interesting, crazy and beautiful Warsaw can be. You start to discover all these nice places.

What is the climate like in Warsaw these days, does the political turmoil affect everyday life?

It has been going on for years now, but it seems like it's getting worse. The right-wing government controls almost all the media and is imple- menting laws trying to tinker with our freedom, for instance when it comes to the internet. It has not yet really affected our everyday life here in Warsaw, but it will in the future. But we're not alone with this kind of right-wing shift—sadly it's happening all over the world these days.

Lets dive into your field of expertise. What's the state of Warsaw nightlife?

Well it's booming in a way. We have a lot of great electronic music festivals around Warsaw throughout the summer. But when it comes to the club scene it's more difficult, because there is a huge turnover. So while there are many nice places in Warsaw that occasionally throw good parties, there is no good perma- nent club where you can always be sure it will be good. In the summer there are a lot of good parties happening in the bars and clubs on the Powiśle riverbank. For instance at *Barka*. Then you have the club *Miłośċ* and of course the infamous after hour club *Luzztro*. They also sometimes have good parties at *Dzik*—a very nice place, with many different things happening there. Then you have *Iskra*, but it's more for house and hip hop. The Palace of Culture also houses two interesting locations for live music, parties or just a drink or two—*Bar Studio* and *Café Kulturalna* are cool, because of the building they're in. Then, *Królikarnia* is a nice place in the park —friends of mine run parties called "Światło" there in the morning.

Are there any good record stores in Warsaw?

You have to go to *Side One*, it's the best place for electronic music in Poland. It's run by friends of mine and you can spend hours sorting through their records. And another good one for vinyl is *Asfalt*, next to club Miłośċ, an offspring of a famous Polish hip-hop label.

What bars and restaurants should we hit before clubbing?

The restaurant and bar scene is exploding in Warsaw and it's hard to keep up with all the new places. Very popular is *Beirut*, a bar and hummus place, with good music taste. There are lots of great bars on or near Oleandrów street where I have my studio. *Bar Małe Piwo*, with a nice beer selection, the dive bar *Oleandrów 3 + Inne Beczki*, *Pozytywy*, and the tapas bar

The wall of the smoking room at Plan B has witnessed the beginning and end of many a Warsaw night out

Bardziej
Centre

Plan B
Centre

Cuda na Kiju
Centre

Zamieszanie
Centre

Prasowy
Centre

Mod
Centre

Ministerstwo Kawy
Centre

Café Me+Me
Centre

Bardziej. Then you have the popular *Plan B*, which is the perfect starting point for a night out, or *Cuda na Kiju* and *Zamieszanie*, which are in the same building and look almost like mirror images of each other. They also have good pizza and other snacks. I am a big fan of our "milk bars", a holdover from Communist Warsaw. I go to *Prasowy* at least two times a week. Good, honest and incredibly cheap food. Then you have *Mod*, which has excellent ramen and donuts. *Ministerstwo Kawy*, the Ministry of Coffee, has the best coffee in town. And *Café Me+Me* is also good for hot beverages.

Any markets to visit?
The *Nocny Market* is a night market on the abandoned platforms of a train station with great food stands. Then there are a few *"Breakfast Markets"* on the weekend, and I especially like the one in Żoliborz. And if you want to shop for Communist memorabilia among lots of other stuff, the *Zoo Market* is a safe bet.

And how about to discover the great outdoors?
That's almost the best thing about Warsaw. We have 76 parks, which tear through the whole city. Take a bike and discover all these nice places. I like to start at *Łazienki Park* and go north through the lovely Mariensztat quarter, all the way up to the *Cytadeli Warszawskiej*, a 19th-century fortress in Żoliborz. If you want to go even further, go to *Las Bielański*, a nice forest.

The interior of Side One might be tiny, but its musical selection will take you on a voyage through time and space

What you should also do is rent a kayak up the river and then go down with it, it is really beautiful and rewarding. The river is really buzzing in the summer—with the beaches along the riverbank, it's really happening.

But are there also good spots for swimming in the Vistula?
No, please don't do that. It is dangerous and dirty.

Where would you go on a day trip out of town?
Going to Kozienice is quite nice. There is a nice castle and lots of sights. The city has a lot of history, so it is a trip for taking in some Polish culture.

Speaking of culture, what are Warsaw's best museums and galleries?
I like *Galeria Foksal*, a modern art gallery. The *Muzeum Wojska Polskiego*, a military museum, might be interesting to learn about Poland's crazy past.

What would be the perfect soundtrack for Warsaw?
Definitely the works of jazz musician and film composer Krzysztof Komeda.

Finally, what's missing from Warsaw?
The things that are missing from Warsaw are exactly what make Warsaw special.

Square Dance
The battle for the soul of Warsaw
Alex Webber

A lot can change in sixteen years. Take Warsaw. When I first arrived here, at the start of the millennium, it was a rundown city that had its eye on the future while being anchored by its past. In a way, that still holds true today, and there's few better examples than the area around Plac Grzybowski.

It was round there I first settled, namely in the faceless oblong blocks that begin on the fringes of the square. Some 19 of these 15-storey buildings once constituted the Żelazna Brama estate: a postwar project designed for 25,000 residents. Built in the 1960s, it was presented as proof of Poland's postwar resurgence. In a war-torn city, it's not hard to understand how it offered a ray of hope for a better future.

As a home I found it glum, however. Constructed using similar techniques as WWII bunkers, my corridors were dark and long and smelled of boiled cabbage. One time, returning from Christmas in England, I came home to find my 60-year old landlord on the sofa in his underpants. "I needed to get away from the wife," he explained meekly. But there was a saving grace to living there—the view. Right down upon Plac Grzybowski.

This had been the melting pot of Warsaw, a place where, during the city's pre-war heyday, Jewish life thrived alongside Russian and Polish. An important trade centre, it was alive in the 19th century with a babble of European tongues. At a time when inter-community relations weren't always the most cordial, Grzybowski was universal. It was a place to meet, trade, live and worship.

Traces of the latter survive, notably in the All Saints' Church at the bottom of the square. Completed in 1893, its breathtaking interiors are festooned with Catholic bling. Evidence of its continued importance can be seen on weekends, when solemn services are conducted for crowds of all ages dressed in their Sunday best.

With a lower profile, the honey-coloured Nożyk Synagogue lies to the west of the square, accessible via a couple of tight, twisty turns through back-alley carparks. Had I not lived next door it might have taken me years to unearth. Warsaw's pre-war Jewish population, the largest in the world after New York, was all but wiped out during the war. But Nożyk— the only synagogue in the capital to survive the Nazis—has been central to the community's rebirth.

This is partly thanks to Michael Schudrich, a New Yorker who is now Poland's Chief Rabbi. Open and accessible, he has seen the synagogue flourish. "When I arrived in this country" he says, "the first job was to actually find if there were any Jews left! But not only did we discover greater numbers than we ever imagined, we found they actually wanted to be Jews." With more and more Poles rediscovering their roots, Schudrich's work has not been short on bizarre incidents. "One devout couple used to be skinheads," he laughs. "Just imagine—from skinheads to covered heads!"

Schudrich is often found meeting and greeting people on the doorstep, and that's especially true on Sabbath when Warsaw's growing Jewish population converges. It's almost a shock when you first see Jews of all generations appear en masse. Close by, a small kosher store plies a busy trade, while placards outside do a bilingual job of introducing Judaism. Every time I pass it, it fills me with hope and optimism.

But to sugar coat it all would be a mistake. As things stand, the future of the nearby Jewish Theatre—the only one in the world to regularly perform in Yiddish—hangs in the balance. Why? Because Warsaw wants a new skyscraper. The dramatists have recently found themselves locked out of their spiritual home by the owners, real-estate firm Ghelamco. Having reneged on a promise to include *Teatr Żydowski* in their new gleaming tower—despite a legal obligation—the property giant has swiftly emptied the theatre and surround it with fences.

"We have a notarial deed that states a Jewish theatre should always exist on this site," says the director Golda Tencer. "We owe our fight to all those here before us, who walked around Plac Grzybowski, worked here, lived, loved and were later murdered in the Holocaust." The fight has taken to the streets, literally. Days after eviction, the company staged a three-day run of "Fiddler on the Roof" on the square, drawing hundreds of spectators. The performances took place on a spot once the corner of the Ghetto. Under the amber summer sunset, it was spine-tingling to watch.

But the Jewish Theatre is not the only venue that faces the axe of gentrification. On the other side of the same building lies *Pardon, To Tu*. And the bulldozers are threatening what is one of the city's most revolutionary music spaces. For an outsider it might be difficult to comprehend the furore. The building is an unremarkable, squat, smeared relic dating from the 1960s. But this is not a struggle over architecture; it's a struggle over culture. To be precise, it's culture versus commercialism.

Everyone remembers their first visit to Pardon, To Tu. On mine, an Ethiopian jazz star played an analogue synthesizer with vocal accompaniment from a glittery 70-year-old Polish chanteuse. I might be wrong though. Memories are easily muddled in Pardon, a tight space framed by scarlet walls clad with album sleeves and books. You leave with hazy recollections of improvised jazz jams and avant-garde blues. "When we opened in 2011," says owner Daniel Radtke, "I wanted to show people a different side to music—not the stuff they can hear every day on the radio."

As he languidly puffs on a cigarette, Daniel's eyes tell the story of a thousand late nights. But if he's bothered by the imminent demise of Pardon, he doesn't show it. "When we signed the contract, we always knew we'd have to leave one day to make way for a skyscraper. If anything, I'm surprised we've actually lasted so long. Of course, privately, I have to ask if the area needs another building like that. To me, it just feels that all the changes are being made for the benefit of the sort of people who never worry about money."

The gentrification was perhaps ignited by the square's redevelopment. An overgrown park was reinvented in 2010 as a shining plaza filled with water features, benches, granite and greenery. At the time I thought replacing trees with concrete was half mad. But the style and sensitivity with which it was done has breathed life into the square, while maintaining the sense of a secret garden.

More changes followed: global architect Helmut Jahn recently added an epic residential tower soaring 40 storeys into the air. Unlike many of Warsaw's recent architectural blunders, this one feels classic and considered rather than a maniacal ego trip. But it's not just the skyline Jahn has shaken up. Ground-floor units include a ceviche bar, an upmarket winery and a "chocolate boutique". To think that back in my day retail opportunities were limited to industrial cleaning products and used washing machine parts.

A few such stores survive, namely on Kamienica Brenkina, a small parade below a faithfully restored three-storey tenement. Passing pedestrians can browse displays of mops, spanners and other household hardware, a throwback to a time when small family businesses ruled the district. But who needs such items now? Not the new breed of locals, anyway. Find them across the square, where new cafés and restaurants have squeezed out the old.

Charlotte, an upmarket boulangerie, is a case in point. Despite the elaborate inkings and piercings of the staff, the clientele are not hipsters. Instead, this is where Warsaw's new money gathers: airhead models and hotshot lawyers who wear red trousers at the weekend. Outside, sports cars and jeeps stand higgledy-piggledy, parked with just a cursory acknowledgment of the outside world.

Splicing this side of Grzybowski in half is Próżna Street, the only street of the Jewish Ghetto that wasn't flattened by the Nazis. For years it was emblematic of Warsaw's urban decay; a dank, derelict alley. Walking it at night I'd often pause to soak in the scene. Rotting walls propped up by wooden scaffolding. Deathly quiet, not a soul in sight. You could almost hear the ghosts of the past whispering in the shadows. Yet now Próżna has been rebooted as a street of brash brasseries and bistros proffering premium champagne. It feels elegant; Parisian almost.

But the question many are asking is, has this all been too much, too soon? Will locals be exiled by rising prices? And in the meantime, a once overlooked, grubby part of town has become not just the centre of a tug-of-war between different social groups, but a mandatory stop on the tourist trail. No other neighbourhood packs in so many layers of history in so few square metres: a Catholic bastion next to a Jewish synagogue; Tsarist tenements next to capitalist fortresses and the dreary Commie blocks I once called home. Most of all though, Grzybowski is evidence that the Nazis didn't succeed—not in eradicating Judaism, and not in eradicating Warsaw. No matter what the future holds, that's good enough for me.

Alex Webber has lived in Warsaw for 16 years, serving since 2011 as the editor-in-chief of the monthly "Warsaw Insider". His work has been featured in The Guardian" and "The Times"

Photo: Helmut Jahn's Cosmopolitan Twarda 2/4 tower soars over the condemned building containing Pardon, To Tu and the Jewish Theatre

Snap Happy

Zuza Krajewska

She's a photographer and filmmaker, treading the fine line between art and fashion. No matter what subject she zooms in on—whether a stylised set for a brand or a series on people with visible marks from injuries—she always works to capture the human essence. Zuza's pictures have fronted top fashion magazines and been exhibited throughout Europe

The multiple reconstructions of Warsaw have provided fertile ground for the artist; epitomised by Zuza, who chose it over New York and London. From her favourite vegan lunch and the best vodka spot to architectural treasures and Varsovian fashion, the photographer trains her lens on the Polish capital

You often work in London and New York. What made you choose Warsaw as your primary base?

Warsaw is very pleasant and convenient. I like its hustle and bustle. There are new interesting places opening constantly for a lovely night out with friends. And you can have a detached house with a garden almost in the centre—an advantage over London.

Travelling so much, it must be easier to recognise the peculiarities of home. What is typical Warsaw?

Everything is nearby. Although it is a big city, there is less traffic than London. The most typical feature is its constant development; the whole city is under construction; everything is changing. That's what I find most appealing.

Is there something that Warsaw lacks?

The smell of the sea where I come from. I was born in Gdańsk on the coast. It's still in my opinion the best place to play truant.

In which part of the city do you live—and why?

I live directly in the city centre. It used to be a red light district, full of prostitutes and thieves. Gentrification has made it a luxurious area with cafés, studios, hotels and restaurants. Everything I need is located within a 500-metre walking distance from my flat, including my studio.

What does your typical day look like?

Breakfast with my daughter, Lula. Lunch at *Tel Aviv* restaurant where they serve gluten-free and vegan food. My favourite places include *Mozaika* for beef tartare and vodka; *Beirut* for hummus; *Kraken Rum Bar* for seafood; *Shoku* for sushi; *Wi-taj* for Thai food; *Burger Bar* for burgers; and *La Sirena* for Mexican food.

You express yourself visually; if you had to represent Warsaw with one snapshot, what would it be?

The artificial palm tree at Rondo de Gaulle'a—by the artist Joanna Rajkowska. I think it represents the Varsovian sense of humour. During years of occupation, the ability to pick up on the absurd gave people strength, hope and a little joy. The best way to undermine the occupant was to use humour as a weapon—though it had to be done cleverly. You can see traces of it in Polish movies.

What about Warsaw inspires you?

The architecture, the clothing style, the housing estates—and older ladies' chic.

Is there a nice gallery or museum for photo and film exhibitions?

We still don't have an institution specialised in photography. *The National Museum* has a wonderful collection but no condition to present it. Fortunately private initiatives arecovering the gap, like the foundation *Archeology of Photography*, which is run by real specialists. In Warsaw you can see interesting work, not just photos, at the *Museum of Modern Art*, though it's temporarily closed. *Galeria Raster* is a pioneer of Central European art. *Foksal* focuses on highlighting radical approaches to contemporary art. It's not-for-profit, so they can avoid pressure from the market and gallery owners. *Leto Gallery* hosts multi-disciplinary events, and *Piktogram* calls itself a "Bureau of Loose Associations". *Królikarnia* sculpture park is magical: a palace in a wild green space. And don't miss *Griffin Art Space*: a hub of art spaces in a post-industrial setting. I'm holding my show "Imago" there.

What other galleries and museums are worth a visit?

Two places especially worth visiting are the *Warsaw Rising Museum* and the Museum of the History of Polish Jews, *Polin*. It stands in what was once the Jewish neighbourhood, and then the Ghetto. Both present an important and transformative aspect of Warsaw's history. For me, the exhibitions are memorable and thought-provoking.

You are an art insider; how is the Warsaw art scene different from London or NYC?

The Warsaw art scene and market—in the Western sense—is quite a young phenomenon. Before 1989, everything—from selling and commission to art criticism—was controlled by the state. In the 1990s we started adopting Western rules, step by step. Now after 25 years Poland is an integral part of the global circuit. The art is bought and shown because of its quality. The main difference from London and NYC is that we are doing many things "for the first time".

And how about fashion?

We don't have globally recognised fashion designers. Everything here is on a smaller scale. *Ania Kuczyńska*'s store is nice. It's the store of the label. Actually, I'm more into labels than stores. You can buy Le Petit Trou lingerie at *Horn&More*, but also online. MISBHV also mostly sells online. And UEG closed their Warsaw store to become more international. That's happening with many brands. Their products sell well abroad, and a store makes less financial sense, as the nice spots are expensive, and many young people prefer online.

What does a day off look like?

I spend time with my baby daughter and with friends, in *Super Salon*—the most up-to-date and reliable bookstore in town. Or a date with my boyfriend Adam—maybe steak tartare at Mozaika.

If you had a weekend to show around a friend what would you do?

I'd take them to *Miłość* ("Love") or one of the bars on the Vistula River bank, like *Cud nad Wisłą*, *Barka* or *Plażowa*. All those places are a 10-minute walk along the riverbank. *Miami Wars* also. Besides having a grill bar they offer a motorboard cruise along the river. Great choice for summer in the city. On Saturday we could have a nice picnic in a park or a garden. We have garden plots in the middle of the city. I'd take them for ice drip coffee to *Emesen* which is a coffee bar, gallery and bookstore in one and show the *Palace of Science and Culture* and the *MDM Hotel* building. Perhaps the *Koło Bazar* flea market too.

Your work contains a documentary approach; what areas of Warsaw are interesting from that perspective?

Housing estate Przyczolek Grochowski. Umschlagplatz, from where the Nazis deported the Jews. From the 1950s central district through the Old Town, rebuilt from the ashes of the war, and the wild river bank, the city has lots to discover. From a documentary point of view don't miss Praga dis-trict and Zbawiciela Square where you can feel the young heart of Poland.

What is the city's essence?

Warsaw defies any definitions.

Above: With an interior as impressive as its exterior, Polin Jewish Museum was European Museum of the Year for 2016
Below: Polish multimedia artist Oskar Dawicki portrays his own death at a recent exhibition for Galeria Raster

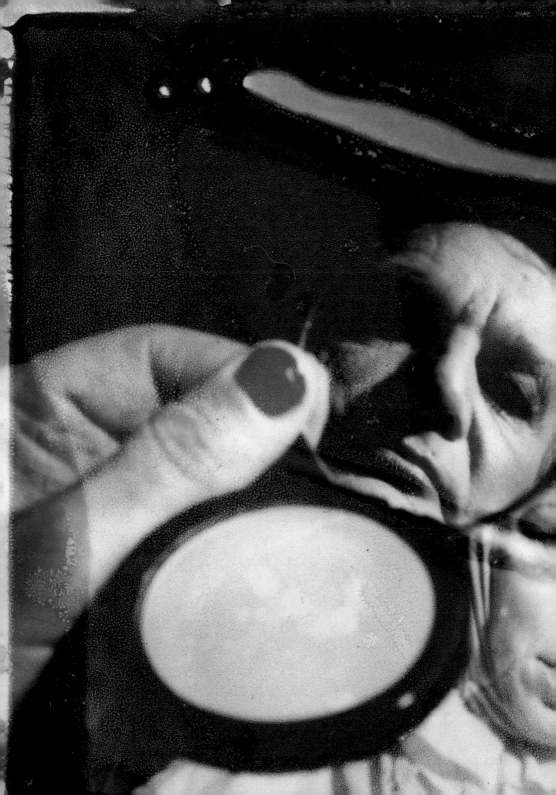

Walk the Line

A showcase by Maciek Nabrdalik

In 2012, the Miss Trans beauty pageant took place in Warsaw, a liberal stronghold in one of Europe's most devoutly Catholic countries. Documentary photographer Maciek Nabrdalik—with World Press Photo and Picture of the Year awards under his belt—was there to document the contest with his 1965 Polaroid. The images were processed using image-transfer and have not been digitally altered

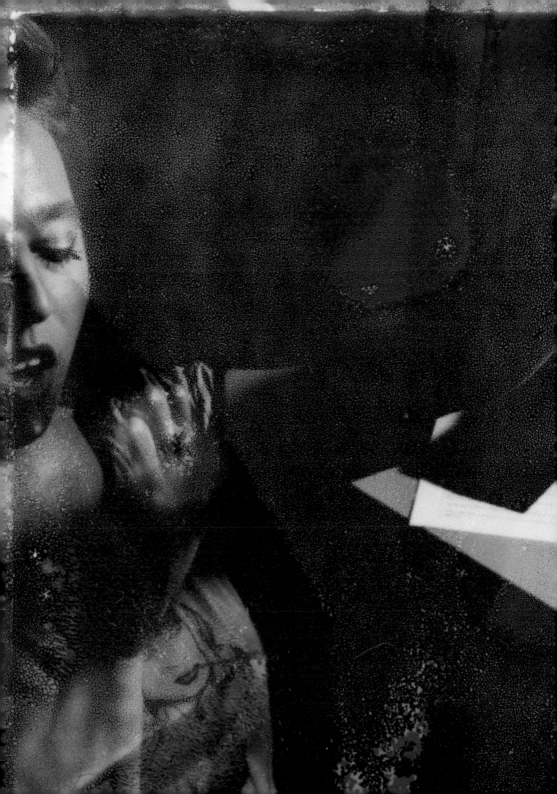

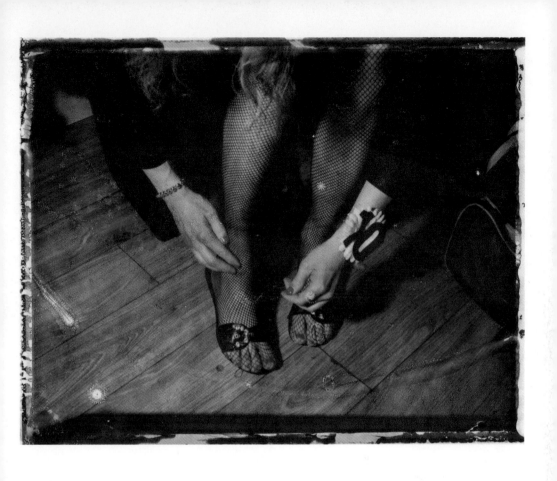

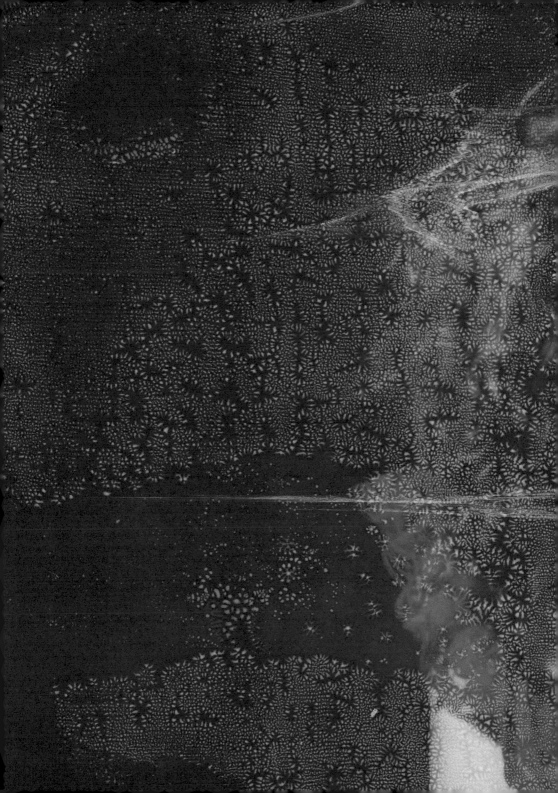

Grzegorz Kwapniewska, Butcher

Prime Cuts

<u>Grzegorz Kwapniewska</u>
He is known in Warsaw restaurants as the "Crazy Butcher"—but it wasn't always that way. Starting out as a hospital consultant, Grzegorz found his true calling and was the first man in town to dry-age meat. Today he supplies quality cuts to over 60 restaurants, including some of the city's finest kitchens

Connected with a network of Warsaw chefs, Grzegorz is the fellow to lead us through the city's exploding dining scene. He reveals the pick of both new and established kitchens, shares where to drink a cocktail made from rice—and gives a primer on how to fill your shot glass with the good stuff

How did you become the "Crazy Butcher"?

When I started learning about meat, I asked lots of people how they prepared it, and researched a lot in books and online. When Daniel Pawełek opened Butchery and Wine he brought his best friend from London, chef Ollie Couillaud. I used to go every day, and I kept asking him, "What are you doing with that", "What are you doing with that"... Once I came in and Ollie said "Oh, it's the Crazy Butcher, hello!" and I thought it was a good nickname!

What is the state of Warsaw dining?

It's very interesting, because it has just changed. A few years ago it was very simple... They just copied things other chefs made. But now a lot of people have come from abroad with new ideas, and they're trying to find local versions of these ideas. So you can find really interesting places, interesting concepts. Many people are going to the restaurants, the service has improved... Still now nobody in New York is saying "Let's eat something good, we'll find it in Warsaw". But I believe in a few years it might happen.

Where in the city can you find the good restaurants?

There's a special thing here. If you go to the main square or streets, you won't find a very good kitchen. The best restaurants are in backyards, back streets.

So what are the best kitchens?

Senses is a really, really good restaurant, which just won what is only the second Michelin star in Warsaw. *Dyletanci* is a new restaurant with a very nice chef who was running Tamka 43 before. You can get really good food there. Rafał Hreczaniuk, the guy responsible for this restaurant, goes around the whole of Poland to find good supplies and brings them 300 or 400 kilometres to Warsaw. *Kieliszki na Próżnej* is actually more of a wine bar with some food, but it's very, very good. And at *Alewino*, the chef is from Italy and also France, so it's rather Mediterranean. *Tamka 43* is a restaurant where you choose from two or three propositions and they give you everything, point by point, with a very nice selection of paired wines. *Butchery and Wine* is a very classic steak house—I think one of the best. And I have to mention one more—*Dyspensa*. It's not very well known, but the people who know it have kept going back for ten years.

What about for traditional Polish food?

The restaurant inside *Wilanów Palace* just outside Warsaw has something really rare. The chef is crazy about traditional food so they search for old recipes and use historical cookbooks. There, you can eat traditional dishes that nobody eats any more in Warsaw. This is inside the palace of one of our kings—and the *Poster Museum* is next to it. For variations on Polish food, try *Solec 44*. It's not strictly traditional, because the chef Aleksander Baron adds strange things. But he uses Polish products and concepts. *Różana* is the third one, this is traditionally Polish. *L'Enfant Terrible* also—Michał Bryś makes traditional cuisine but with a little dash of molecular gastronomy. Just a dash so it's very nice.

And the best pierogi?

Zapiecek is well known—it's a chain, but they do it very well. For other classic dishes, try *Delicja Polska*.

And when you're with the wife and kids?

Again, Solec 44 has a very nice concept. They have games inside—you can play, you can eat. The chef is very creative so you never know what you'll receive. My wife says Aleks is the one person in the world who can take five things she hates and make a dish she loves. It's also great for cocktails. There is a crazy bartender there who makes cocktails from grain, from rice, from everything. You won't get his cocktails anywhere else in the world. Another place for the family is *Jeff's*. It's a normal restaurant. It's not super high cuisine, but they've got very nice pork ribs.

What about for an ice cream?

The best known is *Sucré* in Plac Zbawiciela. The ice creams are totally hand-crafted and there's always a line outside. *Odette* is the best for sweet pastries.

And a good cup of coffee?

Trzecia Waza. It's not a café, it's a burger bar. But they have a great selection of coffees.

What else do you do in your spare time?

Well, it's sailing—but not in Warsaw.

If you had some friends visiting, what would you do?

I'd start by showing them the Old City of course. If we're going to a restaurant, it depends... But there are a few places to find a few options like Poznańska Street, where you have *Beirut* and other good restaurants. For clubs it's Mazowiecka Street. I'd show them the Royal Castle, and probably I'd drive them to Wilanów Palace.

And if you fancied live music?

Tygmont Jazz Club was one of the best jazz clubs in Eastern Europe, during Communist times. Many well known jazz musicians play there and there's excellent jam sessions. You have to be careful which door you're opening as there's a strip club next door!

Any Polish wine you'd recommend?

Polish wines are getting better but we've just started. Four or five years ago there were just a few wineries. So they are in the position of good German wines, with the same grapes... It might change in 10–20 years because the weather is changing. There are some wineries worth trying, but I would concentrate on other alcohol in Poland. One of course is vodka. This is a big industry, and something went in the wrong direction. Everybody tries to distil it three times, four times, six times—so the vodka is cleaner, but with no taste. Then, one distillery director decided, "I won't do it in that way, I will distil it once, and I'll find the best potatoes, the best grain for this. This vodka is Młody Ziemniak, which means young potatoes. The different years' versions give you a totally different flavour. Finding a new way of preparing vodka in a country where everybody knows vodka—this is an art. Our other specialty is "nalewka". I know one of the best nalewka makers in Poland. The drink is made from fruit, but the key is where you get the fruit. So this guy goes all over the country to get different fruit. He might travel 300km to get cherries because those cherries are the best. The man's name is Zbigniew Sierszuza. He can't actually sell his nalewka publicly, because in Poland the license is very expensive. But sometimes you can get it from somebody... Another

A former director and now a star TV chef, Michał Bryś offers unorthodox creativity at L'enfant Terrible

thing you won't find in many countries is the fermented honey wine "myud".

Do bars sell myud and nalewka?
Some yes, some no. But restaurants usually do. I believe at Senses you can get it.

How would you improve Warsaw?
First of all I'd allow restaurants in the Old City to stay open later than 10pm. Somebody had the crazy idea that if you want to live in that area, you shouldn't be outside at night. I can't imagine Amsterdam closing at 10, or London... But in general I think the city is going in the right direction—I wouldn't make a revolution. This city was a little artificial, after the Second World War—people came from different parts of Poland. You need time to become one with Warsaw. When you start living here, you think, "Oh it's flat, there's no sea, lakes, mountains or hills..." So many people—I was one of them—complain that other cities are nicer. But after a few years you start to like the city. It's changing very slowly but constantly. A few more years and it will be a very, very nice place.

Powiśle
By the Riverside

The Vistula bank was a haven for the poor before ambitious city planners revamped the area. Now it's staked its claim as the pulse of the city's summer nightlife—with plenty to discover inland too

Outdoors · Night	Decking Out

History courses through Warsaw along Poland's longest river, the Vistula. It was a crucial trade artery for centuries and a wartime battle line. As recently as 2015 its levels dropped to reveal Jewish tombstones used postwar to shore up the banks, and a Soviet fighter plane—with the pilot still in it. A more prosaic battle ensued this century when local politicians campaigned to reform the "city facing the river"—vis à vis developing the riverside into a living part of Warsaw. Finally in the last few years, this seems to have happened, and the left bank has become a go-to spot for drinks and music. The partymongers behind

downtown watering hole Plan B are some of the pioneers behind the change, setting up floating bar *Barka*. Free entry, surprisingly high quality music, and close proximity mean you can spend an evening exploring the party vessels, including *Hocki Klocki*, *Cud nad Wisłą* and more. If the decks are too crowded, or your sea legs fail you, there's plenty of bars on the banks, though the music might stray more into cheese and locals' approaches might become a little brusque. Look out for waterborne venues on the other side too.
• Powiśle, various locations, see Index p. 64

| **Backstreet Art**

Some places in Warsaw are hard to find. They tend to be in back courtyards, down alleyways and around corners. That's true of *Galeria Foksal*, but it doesn't take a straightforward approach to art either. Since its founding in 1966, artists have always been intrinsically involved in the curation of the exhibitions. For that reason the gallery remains highly respected in creative circles. Still, free entry and a relaxed vibe make it an easy stop for the travelling culture buff. Not to be confused with the Foksal Gallery Foundation, established by a breakaway clique of members pursuing a different direction.
• Galeria Foksal, Ulice Foskal 1/4, galeriafoksal.pl

Food | **Metamorphosis**

Mingle with Warsaw's younger bohemia over board games and books at cosy *Kawiarnia Kafka*, perched upon a park. Simple sandwiches and fresh salads accompany a wide selection of drinks and coffee, all reasonably priced. Lingering is encouraged, with an array of books in many languages as well as toys for the little ones and games for the bigger ones. Lounge chairs dot the lawn across the street, where you can take your coffee and snuggle into a blanket to watch the sun travel across the Warsaw sky.
• Kawiarnia Kafka, Oboźna 3, kawiarnia-kafka.pl

Food · Night | **Day and Night**

...is the motto proclaimed by *Na Lato* on its neon sign. Sitting as it does on charming Park Marszałka Rydza-Śmigłego—with a smooth, fairy-lit deckchair area, tasty pizzas, a famed lamb shank and a range of cocktails—it seems to deliver on the promise. But you can push the "night" part even further next door at *Syreni Śpiew*. Behind the original mosaic façade, inside a faithfully adapted 1970s modernist building, you're likely to find live music and livelier people, lubricated by over 100 types of whisky.
• Na Lato, Rozbrat 44A, na-lato.com; Syreni Śpiew, Szara 10a, syrenispiew.pl

Through the Keyhole

A small open kitchen allows diners to peep in at the chefs preparing their homemade pasta dishes. And therein lies the provenance of the name: *Dziurka od Klucza*, or "keyhole". It might be wise to book a table at this tiny eatery, or risk missing out on stars like pappardelle with honey chicken, or seppia spaghetti with seafood. If you still have room, be sure to taste their homemade cakes and pies. Herbivores will find a tasty alternative just a few metres down this sleepy street at the frankly-named *Veg Deli*.
• Dziurka od Klucza, Radna 13, dziurkaodklucza.com.pl; Veg Deli, Radna 14

Culture · Shop | Défense d'Afficher

When Communist censorship prohibited "Western-style" designs for posters, Varsovians let their imaginations run wild across an essentially uncontrolled medium. And one of the broadest collections of Polish poster art is to be found in the cavernous interior of the university library at *Galeria Plakatu*. Movies, theatre troupes, circus acts and live gigs are all represented with avant-garde shapes and trippy colours. Perfect for your wall, a meaningful gift, or just a long browse through the modern creative history of Poland.
• Galeria Plakatu Włodka Orła, Dobra 56/66, poster.pl

Shop | Magic Wardrobe

Laying claim to an entire retail type through name, it's just as well *Vintage Store* is the only vintage store in Powiśle worth talking about. Rammed with hot finds like Hermés scarves fit for Jackie Onassis, bombers adorned with Picasso, hand-painted leather jackets, lurex disco wear, rare 1990s Moschino pieces and an Adidas collection that'll rival any local hooligan, it's little wonder they have to constantly migrate stock come sale time to a second garage location close by at Lipowa 5 (pictured).
• Vintage Store, Ulica Dobra 56/66, vintagestore.pl

Brick in the Wall

Self-proclaimed as a "hobby gone mad" is street-art shop *Wawa Bla Bla*, the brainchild of British emigrée Gilly Boelman. Not only does it present framed photos—taken by her—of choice pieces of wall material, but frequent collaborations with local artists result in one-off graphic pieces that can provide a memento of the living expression of the street. Internationally recognised artists frequent the store, and have even been known to paint murals outside it.
• Wawa Bla Bla, Dobra 15, wawablabla.pl

Outdoors | Over Books

The jaw-dropping façade of Marek Budzyński's *Warsaw University Library* hardly seems to communicate a harmonious relationship of human with nature. But walk through its giant pod-like interior to reach one of Europe's largest roof gardens, and you might reconsider. Landscape architect Irena Bajerska is behind the one-hectare expanse of falling greenness punctuated by domes, waterfalls and hidden corners—and equipped with sweeping vistas of the city and its murky Vistula. Large pipes and vents intertwine with the botany to conjure a steampunk feel.
• Warsaw University Library, Dobra 56/66, buw.uw.edu.pl

Night | Slow Life

Follow a neon sign up a hill beside the elevated railway to find Alexander Baron's pioneering contribution to the Warsaw slow food movement. Time dilates as you step into *Solec 44*'s homey rooms, where jars of homemade preserves and pickles line the walls alongside all sorts of board game. The talented bartender wields a selection of house syrups that make for inspired cocktails, like white pepper and basil or red berries and mint. The dim terrace is ideal for warmer nights, while the back room might contain surprises like a folk music session. Make it a first stop for a Powiśle night out and expect a mixed, happy crowd.
• Solec 44, Solec 44, solec.waw.pl

Jakub Szczesny
and Marta Wójcicka
Jakub is an architect who toes
the line of artist, pushing
expectations of space. He has
his own studio, SZCZ, and is
part of the collective Centrala,
while his work is scattered
throughout Warsaw and
worldwide. Marta manages
theatre space Teatralne Koło
and design festival Przetwory,
as well as working with Polish
institutions and collaborating
with her husband

Jakub Szczesny & Marta Wójcicka, Architect & Cultural Manager

Walk in the Park

With long-term roots in the area of Saska Kępa, not much happens there that Marta doesn't know about; while Jakub's upbringing in Ursynów, and his 30 subsequent addresses, provide another perspective. The pair share the best bakeries, a secret-garden restaurant, top parks and architectural highlights—along with plenty of history

Where in Warsaw do you both live—and why?

Marta: I was born here in Saska Kępa. I'm third generation; my grandmother was born here. Pre-war this was a residential place, and after the war it became more posh. It was full of home-owners as well as artists—a lot of painters and sculptors lived here, so it has a really nice history for me. Plus it's very close to the centre—cross Poniatowski Bridge by foot and you're exactly in the centre.

Jakub: Everything is within walking distance. It's a very safe part of Warsaw, though it's the right bank. It's the niche of the biggest money in the city.

Marta: It has changed a lot. Right now you have a lot more coffee places, restaurants, and a lot of Warsaw people come here on the weekends. It has started to be more trendy. There are parks and green areas so it's great to be here with kids.

Can you talk a little about work?

Marta: We have a space called Studio Teatralne Koło inside *Soho Factory*, an industrial building that also houses a gallery, *Muzeum Neonów* (Neon Museum) and the best coffee in Warsaw—*Kofi Brand*. My second organisation is dedicated to projects related to performance, as well as design and architecture.

Jakub: I'm an architect and artist—interested in what can be broadly called the production of space. I use my tools to explore narratives that regular architecture cannot respond to. My studio's name is SZCZ, and for 15 years I've been working with a critical architecture group that's not about just building but about shaping reality, in terms of public con-sciousness. This is Centrala. We

made "the narrowest house," *Keret House*, in Warsaw.

What does a day off look like?

Marta: Since we had kids, our lives have really changed. I'm an expert on the playgrounds in Warsaw. The best one is *Park Stefana Żeromskiego* in Żoliborz which has the café *Prochownia*, and *Kalimba*, which is a toy shop and café combined. Nearby our home in Saska Kępa we like to go to *Francuska Trzydzieści* for coffee. We also take the kids to get ice cream at the famous *Sosenka*. And a place I recently discovered, *Deseo Patisserie*.

Jakub: And then of course there's the cream rolls from *Irena*.

Marta: It's been around for ages and is one of the last traditional places. You meet old people, young people, hipsters, everyone. They bake on the spot and it is in a beautiful place surrounded by little villas. They have Warsaw's best "makowiec"—traditional Polish poppy seed cake.

Jakub: You also have to eat the "jagodzianki"—a classic summer blueberry cake.

Marta: And next door is *Kwiatkarnia*. The owner is an old lady who has a small house and a huge garden. It's not an official place—you sit in her garden and she brings her cakes. It's very homey, they don't advertise. It's perfect to relax and easy for kids to play.

Jakub: And there's *Lukullus*, which has become a chain. The younger generation took over from their family and made it more dynamic.

Marta: They went to Paris to learn how to make cakes. They've put in a lot of effort and it works.

Jakub: There is also a fantastic playground called *Ogród Jordanowski*, which comes from the 19th-century ideas of Dr. Henryk Jordan.

Broad in cultural outlook, specific in its sourcing of rare titles, Bookoff is a good place to browse, read or think

He started a huge social initiative of building democratic playgrounds. It's beautiful. It has a very interesting community building with a sloped roof for sledge riding.

Marta: One of the most beautiful parks is *Skaryszewski Park*. It's a picnic place because you can lay on the grass next to lakes and beautiful sculptures. Nearby are two great places to eat—*Misianka* has really special cakes and *Dziki Lokator* does small pizzas and snacks in the middle of the park. On the other side of Skaryszewski is another park *Błonia Elekcyjne*. It has a unique landscape with a canal and field.

Jakub: These were the "election fields"—where noblemen met to elect the kings.

Marta: It is a vast landscape and somewhere very far away you see buildings. It is amazing. I don't know of any other cities with such a huge green space. And when the wind is good, you can smell what the Wedel chocolate factory is making.

Can you recommend other sites worth visiting for architecture?

Jakub: You'll see examples of modernist buildings in Saska Kępa and Żoliborz.

Marta: In Saska Kępa there is a building designed by a very special architect Lucjan Korngold—now garden restaurant *Biała*. This is by Grupa Warszawa. They have a bunch of clubs and bars, but each is very different.

Jakub: The *MDM Hotel* in the centre is a good example of socialist realism. Warsaw Old Town is very interesting because it was entirely rebuilt in the 1950s. It's a Disney-esque reinterpretation, because the divisions of narrow spaces are just represented in the façade, but behind you have much bigger houses that don't represent what was there before.

Marta: It's quite abandoned. Warsaw people don't go there.

Jakub: It's a tourist zone, basically. Or old French people would buy apartments in the zone. Lots of people who were involved with the Communist regime received apartments there. And the place has a strange energy, because the Warsaw Uprising happened there. So there's lots of dead bodies buried in the gothic cellars of these buildings. You can smell the karma. But the story is interesting. Two years before the war, an architecture professor felt there was something brewing, so, with his students he made an inventory of the entire Old Town. When the war came, the book was hidden in the library and saved from the Germans. And they managed to convince the Communists to rebuild the thing.

Marta: For architecture, there's also the area of Muranów. We lived there.

Jakub: It was mostly designed by pre-war architects forced to build socialist realism. It sits on hills created by bulldozers that demolished the Ghetto—what remained of the Jewish district. They made their way between piles of rubble, creating fields and hills. When you go there with old Jewish people they weep because they see the names of streets but don't recognise anything. But one of the last surviving 19th-century market halls is there—*Hala Mirowska*. This is where you can buy vegetables straight from the countryside. And of course the *Polin Museum* is there. Plus *Jaś & Małgosia*, a 1960s bar—they kept the original neon but there's a new hipster vibe.

Where can visitors get a feel of the local creative scene?

Marta: Definitely Soho Factory. You can spend a day there eating, looking around, having coffee that's roasted right there. They're putting money into "Creative Praga", which will help build places for artists. On Inżynierska Street you can go from one studio to another. Also on Targowa Street.

Jakub: We're going through a tremendous period of gentrification. It's not New York, but it's going on and it's inevitable. Praga was like The Bronx, but suddenly there's a new railway line being built and things are changing.

Marta: Another creative district is Powiśle, with studios and cafés as well as the *Copernicus Science Centre*.

Jakub: And *Warszawa Powiśle*, a former ticket office that's now a bar, which I designed with some friends. It's originally part of a system of railway buildings. The architects had free rein to experiment with concrete, so they did fantastic things.

Where do you shop for design objects, art books and magazines?

Marta: *Bookoff* is one of the best bookstores, but I also have to mention the best one for kids—perhaps in Europe—*Dwie Siostry*. Their publishing house is responsible for launching many careers, especially illustrators. We also use a website wallbeing.com, which supports young Polish graphic designers. I have to say I think Poland has the best graphic designers.

Jakub: You should visit the *Poster Museum*. We have a strong history with posters, related to the fact we don't use photographs, or this US way of putting faces. We use a higher level of symbolic representation and typography. We're going

Lukullus bakeries are known for freshness and creativity—try the branch at Chmielna 32 for the best matching décor

through a revival of this style, since some of the big 1960–70s names are now teaching.

What are your favourite meals?
    Marta: I love *Krowarzywa*, it's a great veggie bar where you can get vegan burgers. I also love "pączki" pastries—like doughnuts with rose jam inside. *A. Blikle* is the best place to get them. It's a very traditional spot for tourists and old ladies but I love to go there. And the ice creams at *Malinowa*. Also, there is something I loved as a teenager, which you might find in the Old Town. It's called "bulka z pieczarkami"— bread filled with mushroom stew.

And for a weekend trip out of town?
    Marta: I love Podkowa Leśna. It's great, you take the WKD train from the city centre and in 30 minutes you're in a totally different environment. This is where Jakub built a house surrounded by trees. You can also take a bike along the Vistula River to the *Ogród Botaniczny* (botanical garden).

Chopin List

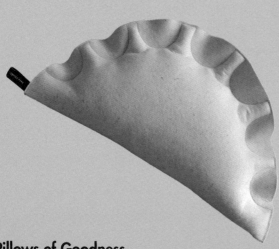

Pillows of Goodness

Empanadas, wantan, dumplings—everyone stuffs their buns. And you can pay homage to the Polish version with this larger-than life pierogi cushion. A definite conversation starter.
• Pierogi cushion, paracollective.com

Oil You Need

Poznań's Alba cosmetics hark back to a lab opened in 1913. When WWII began, owner and chemist Mieczysław Rychlicki saved a book of recipes and a handful of products—enough for his grandson to rebuild the business. Using herbal medicines, essential oils and plant extracts, the products' philosophy is "healthy is beautiful".
• Alba cosmetics, alba1913.pl

Personal Planks

Goodbye, dated off-the-shelf skis—Szymon Girtler hand-crafts next-level planks in his workshop. Ash wood, bamboo, reinforcement materials and some 50 hours of work go into the creations. The honey-coloured results express the natural character of the wood—joining sports tool and design object. Pros can sit down with Girtler to plan a bespoke pair, with weight, height and typical snow conditions factored in.
• Monck Custom Skis, monckcustom.com

Books

Snow White and Russian Red
• Dorota Masłowska, 2002

Masłowska wrote this book when she was 18; a fact which becomes more impressive with every page. Set in millennial, pre-EU Poland, the novel pokes its head expertly into the clouds of social commentary on nationalism, while its feet dangle in drug addiction and the daily lives of Polish white trash.

The Collected Poems: 1956–1998
• Zbigniew Herbert, 2008

The great Herbert might be an obvious choice, but it's impossible to pass over this captivating, eclectic selection. The verses stretch from dark memories of World War II, over the pitfalls of Communist rule, and into the Polish Solidarity movement.

A Memoir of the Warsaw Uprising
• Miron Białoszewski, 1970

An uprising is never a fair fight, but that didn't stop the Warsaw Ghetto militants from fighting the well-oiled German war machine with a few handguns and grenades. They resisted for 63 days and most paid with their lives. Białoszewski's account is deemed the most accurate—and avoids pathos in its brave approach.

Films

Knife in the Water
• Roman Polanski, 1962

The Polish director's first feature film is a tense story of a love triangle—with one notable difference. The whole picture takes place on a boat. Hence the crew were forced to shoot it hanging from the sides of the boat or from a life raft.

Katyń
• Andrzej Wajda, 2007

The Katyn massacre that cost 22,000 Polish military members their lives in 1940 is one of the touchiest subjects in the ever-difficult relationship between Poland and Russia. Wajda's account is as brutal and unapologetic as the tragedy itself and earned him an Academy Award nomination.

Ida
• Paweł Pawlikowski, 2013

The first Polish film to win the foreign language Oscar is the gently haunting story of a young nun in 1962 who discovers she is Jewish. Shot exquisitely in black and white—and with a 4:3 aspect ratio—a richly symbolic cinematic language makes for a timeless masterpiece.

Music

Astigmatic
• Krzysztof Komeda, 1966

Komeda had a prolific, influential career, scoring several of Polanski's films including "Rosemary's Baby", before dying at 37. His greatest legacy might be this modal jazz tour de force, said to have marked a shift from US dominance of the genre.

The Best of Niemen
• Czesław Niemen, 1979

Looking like an outlaw from a Western, this iconic Polish song-smith embodied a freer vision of the nation for generations. Though he later moved into prog rock and jazz fusion, his 1967 protest song "Dziwny jest ten świat" ("Strange is this World") remains an anthem.

Basic Colour Theory
• Catz N' Dogz, 2015

The Polish duo cemented their reputation as dance floor experts with their debut album a decade ago. The long musical road has led to their latest LP—packed with poppy melodies and a brand new approach, and featuring the likes of Green Velvet and Peter, Bjorn and John.

LOST iN

The City

Getting lost in the city is not about throwing away the map
It's about surrendering yourself to the essence of the place
The art and creativity that provide its individual inspiration
The sights, smells, flavours and sounds that make it unique

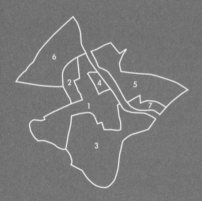

Districts

1/Centre, Ujazdów & Ochota

Luzztro
Aleje Jerozolimskie 6
luzztro.pl
→ p. 10, 15, 23 Ⓝ

Miłość Kredytowa 9
Kredytowa 9
+48 226 572 183
→ p. 23, 32 Ⓝ

Ministerstwo Kawy
Marszałkowska
St 27/35
+48 503 080 906
ministerstwokawy.pl
→ p. 24 Ⓕ

Mod
Oleandrów 8
+48 570 205 746
→ p. 24, 51 Ⓕ

Moko61
Mokotowska 61
+48 226 228 002
moko61.com
→ p. 15 Ⓢ

**Museum of
Modern Art**
Pańska 3
+48 225 964 010
artmuseum.pl
→ p. 31 Ⓒ

**Muzeum Wojska
Polskiego**
Aleje Jerozolimskie 3
+48 226 295 271
muzeumwp.pl
→ p. 25 Ⓒ

National Museum
Aleje Jerozolimskie 3
+48 226 211 031
mnw.art.pl
→ p. 14, 25 Ⓒ

Nocny Market
Kolejowa 8/10A
→ p. 16, 24 Ⓕ

Nolita
Wilcza 46
+48 222 920 424
nolita.pl
→ p. 11, 16 Ⓕ

Nowa Jerozolima
Aleje Jerozolimskie 57
→ p. 8 Ⓝ

Ogród Botaniczny
Prawdziwka 2,
Powsin
ogrod-powsin.pl
→ p. 59 Ⓞ

**Oleandrów 3
+ Inne Beczki**
Oleandrów 3
+48 601 222 114
→ p. 23 Ⓝ

**Palace of Culture
and Science**
Plac Defilad 1
+48 226 567 600
pkin.pl
→ p. 32 Ⓒ

Pardon, To Tu
Plac Grzybowski 12/16
+48 513 191 641
pardontotu.pl
→ p. 28 Ⓝ

Piktogram Gallery
Ulica Kredytowa 9/26
+48 226 241 119
piktogram.org
→ p. 16, 31 Ⓒ

Plan B
Aleja Wyzwolenia 18
+48 503 116 154
→ p. 24, 50 Ⓝ

Pozytywy
Oleandrów 3
+48 510 196 250
→ p. 24 Ⓝ

Prasowy
Marszałkowska 10/16
+48 666 353 776
prasowy.pl
→ p. 8, 24 Ⓕ

Przegryź
Mokotowska 52
+48 226 217 177
→ p. 16 Ⓕ

Restauracja Senses
Bielańska 12
+48 223 319 697
sensesrestaurant.pl
→ p. 47, 49 Ⓕ

Side One
Chmielna 21
+48 228 260 269
sideone.pl
→ p. 23 Ⓢ

Sucré
Mokotowska 12
sucre.pl
→ p. 48 Ⓕ

Super Salon
Chmielna 10
+48 224 681 619
supersalon.org
→ p. 15, 32 Ⓢ

Teatr Żydowski
Plac Grzybowski
12/16
+48 228 505 656
teatr-zydowski.art.pl
→ p. 32 Ⓒ

Tel Aviv Food & Wine
Poznańska 11
+48 226 211 128
→ p. 31 Ⓕ

Tygmont Jazz Club
Mazowiecka 6/8
+48 228 283 409
tygmont.com.pl
→ p. 48 Ⓝ

Weles Bar
Nowogrodzka 11
+48 602 773 997
welesbar.pl
→ p. 10, 16 Ⓝ

Wi-Taj
Plac Konstytucji 2
+48 221 272 123
→ p. 31 Ⓕ

Youmiko Vegan Sushi
Hoża 62
+48 224 046 736
youmiko.vg
→ p. 16 Ⓕ

**Zachęta – National
Gallery of Art**
Plac Małachows-
kiego 3
+48 225 569 600
zacheta.art.pl
→ p. 14 Ⓒ

Zamieszanie
Nowy Świat 6/12
→ p. 24 Ⓝ

Zapiecek
Aleje Jerozolimskie 28
zapiecek.eu
→ p. 47 Ⓕ

Zorza
Żurawia 6
+48 668 401 844
zorzabistro.pl
→ p. 16 Ⓕ

2/Mirów
& Muranów

Fundacja Arton
Miedziana 11
+48 502 055 130
fundacjaarton.pl
→ p. 16 Ⓒ

Griffin Art Space
Miedziana 11
+48 222 121 910
griffin-artspace.com
→ p. 31 Ⓒ

Keret House
Żelazna
kerethouse.com
→ p. 56 Ⓒ

Jaś & Małgosia
Jana Pawła II 57
+48 500 139 352
klubjasimalgosia.pl
→ p. 58 Ⓝ

Polin Museum
Anielewicza 6
+48 224 710 301
polin.pl
→ p. 31, 58 Ⓒ

Red Onion
Burakowska 5–7
+48 228 171 339
redonion.pl
→ p. 15 Ⓢ

Shoku
Karolkowa 30
+48 575 772 500
shoku.pl
→ p. 31 Ⓕ

Starter Gallery
Andersa 13
+48 509 935 632
starter.org.pl
→ p. 31 Ⓒ

**Archeology
of Photography**
Andersa 13
+48 226 281 464
faf.org.pl
→ p. 31 Ⓒ

U Kucharzy
Długa 52
+48 228 267 936
gessler.pl
→ p. 16 Ⓕ

Zoo Market
Aleja Solidarności 55
→ p. 15, 16, 24 Ⓢ

6/Saska Kępa

Biała
Francuska 2
+48 223 072 312
→ p. 57 Ⓕ

Deseo Patisserie
Angorska 27
+48 226 176 304
deseopatisserie.com
→ p. 56 Ⓢ

Francuska Trzydzieści
Francuska 30
+48 530 630 850
→ p. 56 Ⓕ

Irena Cukiernia
Zakopiańska 20
+48 226 172 345
cukierniairena.pl
→ p. 56 Ⓕ

Kawiarnia
Kwiatkarnia
Zakopiańska 24
+48 692 838 661
→ p. 56 Ⓕ

Ogród Jordanowski
Alfreda Nobla 18
+48 226 175 962
→ p. 56 Ⓞ

Pola Magnetyczne
Londyńska 13
+48 605 964 470
polamagnetyczne.
com → p. 16 Ⓒ

Sosenka
Francuska 30
→ p. 56 Ⓕ

7/Żoliborz

Breakfast Market
Aleja Wojska
Polskiego 1
+48 508 121 891
targsniadaniowy.pl
→ p. 24 Ⓕ

Cytadeli
Warszawskiej
Skazańców 25
→ p. 24

Kalimba
Ludwika
Mierosławskiego 19
+48 228 397 560
kofifi.waw.pl
→ p. 56 Ⓕ

Park Stefana
Żeromskiego
Plac Thomasa
Woodrowa
Wilsona 181
→ p. 56 Ⓞ

Prochownia
Czarnieckiego 51
+48 690 900 970
prochowniazoliborz.
com → p. 56

8/Other

Bródno Sculpture
Park
Kondratowisca/
Chodecka, Bródno
artmuseum.pl
→ p. 9 Ⓞ

Koło Bazar
Obozowa 99, Koło
+48 228 362 351
→ p. 32 Ⓢ

Las Bielański
Podleśna, Bielany
→ p. 24 Ⓞ

Poster Museum
Stanisława Kostki
Potockiego 10/16,
Wilanów
+48 228 424 848
postermuseum.pl
→ p. 10, 59, 47 Ⓒ

Oskar Hansen House
Mlekicie 4, Szumin
artmuseum.pl
→ p. 11 Ⓒ

Wilanów Palace
Restaurant
Stanisława Kostki
Potockiego 10/16,
Wilanów
wilanow-palac.pl
→ p. 47 Ⓕ

Available from LOST iN

Next Issue: Zurich

LOSTIN.COM

Najdalszy kurs

NAPISANY PRZEZ JAKUB ŻULCZYK

PÓŁNOC.

DWÓCH FACETÓW NA POSTOJU TAKSÓWEK.

The Farthest Ride

Jakub Żulczyk

Midnight. Two men at a cab stop. A line of cars at the entrance to Wilanowska underground station. A grocery store nearby is closed; a 24-hour off-license with booze and cigs, a bit closer, is open. A heatwave was forecast, but it is terribly windy. There's plenty of space for the fierce wind to bluster—the station entrance, the bus terminal, the stretch of a market place.

Two men at the stop. Not just them, of course—others, too: lazy, tired, smoking, filling in sweepstake coupons, betting on football or horses, listening to the radio, doing crosswords while the younger lot log on to Tinder—but I'm interested in precisely these two: one older, one younger.

"I can't sleep. I'm achy all over. I drove a guy to Poznań yesterday," says the first one—tall, stout, with a good-natured face, short, thinning hair, forty-ish. He lights up and offers the pack to his companion. Shorter, much younger, he grabs one—after a while. He's not too keen on helping himself like that. He has short hair with a side parting and a hoodie which seems small—but perhaps that's how he likes it. Twenty-something, nervous. He keeps jiggling, as if he were awaiting a message which might turn out very good, or very bad. If you approached him, you'd smell his cologne. Strong and sweet, as if he's squirted himself with coloured booze.

The older one looks calmer. He stretches, gripping elbow with hand, as if he had some sort of injury. The younger one looks around, spitting repeatedly. He makes a sound while spitting, like the hissing of a cymbal.

"Me? I've been back and forth to the brothel," he says.

"Ah, right. The NATO summit," replies the older one, in a serious tone.

"Hey, Lech's gonna win, I bet double on Lech!" shouts someone from a car parked further down.

"Shut the fuck up!" shouts the younger one. Then turns to his companion. "He just drove a guy to Lublin for 150 zlotys", he explains. "For fuck's sake! I was ready to smash his windshield with a brick."

The wind, it can drive you crazy. The younger one pulls the hood tight over his head. He flicks his butt, still burning. The spark dances in the air, blown by the wind, like a firefly.

"By the way," asks the older guy. "What was your farthest ride?"

"And you? asks the younger, who likes to ompote All in all, he likes to fight. The older one looks towards the station.

"Well… Sopot, Gdańsk… the likes", he replies.

"Mine was to Rome," grins the younger one.

"You're shitting me." He snorts with incredulity.

"I'm not!" replies the younger one.

"You're shitting me!"

"I'm not! Remember that cloud from Iceland, when the bloody volcano erupted? I was fucking this chick from the Marriott Hotel reception desk at the time, and so she calls me and asks: 'Hey, you. Okęcie Airport's come to a standstill, and I have a guy wants you to take him to Rome. An Eyetie.' I was driving a Vauxhall at the time, a piece of crap. I wouldn't have got as far as Praga."

"The Czech capital," says the fat guy.

"No, the Praga district of Warsaw!" laughs the younger one. He's feeling jolly.

"And?" asks the older one.

"Nothing. The Eyetie says we make no stops and he pays 5,000 euros. I say: 'You pay 8,000, and my mate is coming. I won't make it on my own with no sleep.' And hey, he agreed."

"He must have been a big cheese," nods the older one.

"He sure was. And so we went. Fuck, when I got back my suitcase was all packed, waiting in the hallway. My missus was well pissed off."

They light up again. A dozen people emerge from the station. They vanish in the dark as if they'd never been there, like ghosts. The older guy looks around, fearful, as if he suddenly remembered something forgotten, which he wants to forget again. The younger one spots the change, but says nothing. The older one inhales his smoke and calms down. He claps, all of a sudden, possibly to stop whatever was going on in his head.

"When did you come back then?" he asks.

"After a week," the younger one replies.

"You brought back the cash though, right?" the older one asks.

"Are you kidding? I had five euros on me," the younger one spits, hissing again. Someone is arguing about the betting. Across the road in front of the off-license, two groups of shitfaced youths are slogging it out. Suddenly, one gets kicked in the belly. A loud moan resonates in the air.

"Touring the city, partying hard…" says the older.

"Get the fuck out!" The younger guy watches the skirmish.

"For sure, he'd love to join in," the older one is surely thinking. "He can't keep still. I was the same at his age".

"We stayed in! Rome is bloody expensive," the younger one adds after a while. They both laugh.

And yet again, they flick the cigarette stubs and send sparks floating in the air. The wind blusters more and more.

If you were standing here, you'd certainly look for somewhere to hide. But them—they keep on standing. A long while passes and I see them, from afar, getting in their cars to warm up a bit.

Jakub Żulczyk was born in 1983 in Mazury, and is a Warsaw-based novelist, screenwriter and columnist. His crime TV show "Belfer" (The Teach) screened on Polish Canal+, while his latest novel "Blinded by the Lights" (2014), depicted six days in the life of a Warsaw cocaine dealer and has sold 40,000 copies in Poland. A TV series adaptation co-written by Żulczykis is now in pre-production

LOST iN
FOUND OUT

Experience the city like a local

⊙ **Insider recommendations**
Curated tips from creative locals

🗺 **Interactive map**
GPS your way to the choice spots

☁ **Download for offline use**
Wander free, without roaming

📋 **Create your itinerary**
Save your places, make your trip

LOST iN